T-shirt to Tuxedo

T-shirt to Tuxedo

A Collection of Stories by Tyson Brown, an Ordinary Man

Tyson Brown

Copyright © 2021 Tyson Brown
All rights reserved
ISBN-978-1-7368353-0-2

Cover art by Katie Mefford

TABLE OF CONTENTS

CHRISTY

If this all works out right, your name and this message will be the first published words of mine that anyone reads. As you well know, I'm notorious for things not necessarily working out exactly as I plan, but you also know, I try hard. Nevertheless, without you, there would be no page 1, 2, or whatever the ending page number of this book is. There simply would be no beginning to any of this, and everyone knows you can't have an ending without a beginning. God spoke to me over and over, saying "write the book." You two must have been in cahoots because I'm certain you told me just a few thousand times more than God did. The fact that this is in anyone's hands at all is ONLY because of you. Thanks for continuing to be my nudge.

DEDICATION

This book is merely a retelling of tales. A book dedicated to those who have been participants in my story, some contained within and some not, but all influential in the shaping of my life. To my beautiful bride Christy, without your constant nudging this work would be nothing more than memories lost within my piles of journals. To my kids, Winston, Wyatt, and Akosua, you all provide me with a plethora of material. To my grandparents, parents, family, teachers, farmers, African friends, high school friends, college friends, church friends, single moms, homeless friends, , ex-cons and former drug dealers, carnies, and recovering addicts – all of you have abundantly blessed me with time well spent and a story to tell. Yet a single word will not be remembered if it's not told properly. I must specifically dedicate these stories to the man who I spent my first 40 years trying to keep up with and who taught me from daylight 'til dark how to tell a good story, my grandpa, Melvin Murray.

As you will notice, most of the lessons I learn in my stories are after the fact, sometimes years later, after I've reflected and listened to what God was telling me or teaching me in that moment. As I took time to listen, then I learned. Don't miss a chance to listen to the Holy Spirit as you read the questions at the end of each chapter. They are meant to ponder, provoke, and inspire.

CHAPTER 1

ORDINARY GUY

We need to remember that the disciples were common men given a compelling task...they were an ounce more devoted than they were afraid, and, as a result, did some extraordinary things.[1]

Max Lucado

On January 12, 2009, I woke up, walked into the bathroom, looked in the mirror, and said, *I'm 33 today. Jesus was 33 when he died. What have I done to make His kingdom bigger in my 33 years?* I'm not sure how profound that really was for an ordinary married guy, living in the Bible Belt of rural Oklahoma with two kids and a sometimes beloved beagle. I think I even followed the statement up with, *33, cool, that was Larry Bird's number.* I hadn't a clue that my single statement was going to prove itself much more profound than I had anticipated. Anticipated? I never even thought about anything happening. I was just talking to talk. I don't know if those uttered words were the keys that started God's bus I had involuntarily gotten on, but had I been able to see seven months into the future I would have jumped from it.

On July 5th of that same year my grandmother, Joan Murray, passed away. I spent many a night of my youth at her and my Grandpa Melvin's house in the small south-central town of Maysville, Oklahoma. I lived my entire life in Maysville until moving off to college which was only 50 miles from my rural Oklahoma upbringing. Grandma was a loyal farmer's wife that could love a baby with one hand and chase you out of the kitchen with the wire end of a fly swatter in the other. She was not shy about washing your mouth out with Lava soap if the words you spewed were deemed unacceptable, yet she'd turn right around and feed you an apricot fried pie once you understood the error of your ways. A good woman! (I'm convinced there will be an all-night apricot fried pie stand when we get to heaven.)

The next few days after her passing, I stayed all night with my grandfather. The term staying all night was equivalent to a sleepover in Grandpa's dictionary when I was growing up. I listened to him tell story after story about her, even sharing a pot of coffee at midnight a couple times when he couldn't sleep.

After a little tug from God and a nudge from my beautiful bride Christy, I felt it appropriate to preach my grandma's funeral service. With the blessing of the family, I spent an entire day in the solitude of my parent's country home preparing my words. I felt very confident in what God had laid on my heart to say. What I wasn't confident in was being able to get through the funeral without breaking down. I knew if I looked out and saw my grandpa, then I would completely lose it right in front of everyone.

The church was only designed to comfortably seat maybe 50. My family alone could have packed out the place. It was a standing room only crowd that trailed out through the back of the church. When I finally spoke, well, it was indescribable. The words! In the past, I had taught an adult Sunday school class, and in my excitement of teaching, I would often skip over some of my finer points, but not on this day.

I finished up and sat back with the family as everyone began to pass by and pay their respects. Then, out of nowhere, a guy I'd never seen before in my life leaned into the pew, put his arm around me, and said, *Where are you a minister?*

My answer very clearly was, *Nowhere.*

He then asked, *Have you ever felt the call from God?*

Quickly again I said, *No.*

He then left me with this parting statement, *Well maybe you ought to be praying about that son.*

What? Who was this guy? I knew everybody in that church, but this one guy! And, who was he to ask me that? The audacity! He didn't even know me.

From the other side I got this Hacksaw Jim Dugan-like elbow to the ribs and heard the gentle voice of my loving wife say, *So when are you going to start listening to God? Everybody sees it but you.*

Again! The audacity. But she did know me, all of me.

She had witnessed firsthand some serious change in me that I was paying no attention to whatsoever. However, I should have because God was having me do some really weird things. Weird like, chunk my coveted AC/DC concert t-shirts and pour out perfectly good, smooth bourbon whiskey. I was even teaching Sunday school class at our current church, and in the summer providing a bit of light preaching at the lake to a denominationally mixed group of believers bearing cut-offs, tank tops, and swim suits (I loved that gig by the way).

Christy kept saying, *Are you sure you aren't being called to the ministry?*

To which I always answered, *No.* Mainly because I didn't have a clue what *being called* even meant. The denomination I grew up in didn't use that particular lingo.

After the funeral, I was on a mission to find *This Guy.* I was pushing down little old ladies in my path who were trying to kiss my cheeks in a desperate attempt to track down this phantom complimentor. But he was gone. As quickly as he popped into my life in the fourth row pew, he was out of it. Off we went to family dinner and there he was opening the thing up with prayer. Turns out he was the pastor of the church where my aunt attended.

Once the *Bless this Food* prayer was over, I did what any polite person would do.

I walked right up to him and said, *Hey you! Why did you say what you said?* Very eloquent, I thought.

Over an hour later, *This Guy*, Christy, and I engaged in one of the most uplifting and eye-opening spiritual talks I'd ever experienced in my life. The Lord, through this total stranger, spoke some deep words of wisdom over us that day.

I really don't know where our ministry would be had he not been bold in speaking to me that day. He opened our eyes to the potential of God's plan like no one had before. He instructed us how to handle, together, what he felt God was about to thrust upon us. Trust me when I say there were more than one or two big gulps during this conversation.

Particularly when he mentioned, *Hey, if you ever get a burning in your gut and you gotta get it out, you can preach at my church anytime. Just pick up the phone.*

WOW! *This Guy* had known me for no more than a few hours. I wouldn't have even let him borrow my pocket knife this early in our relationship much less preach at my church, if I had one.

In the coming months, God pressed on me hard through scripture and the message of another pastor who I'd been listening to online. The scripture was Acts 4:13-14 from The Message translation:

They couldn't take their eyes off them—Peter and John standing there so confident, so sure of themselves! Their fascination deepened when they realized these two were laymen (ordinary men) with no training in Scripture or formal education. They recognized them as companions of Jesus...

And within one of the pastor's messages he challenged his staff with this question, *What would you be willing to attempt for God if you knew you couldn't fail?* This completely blew me away when I heard it. It was the most radical Christian thing I had ever heard.

So much that I blurted out, *I'd quit my job and start a church*!

And that's just what we did, with the exception of quitting the job. We started a church in our house that reached out to people who had been burned and hurt by The Church. I don't use the word *we* lightly either. When you enter into ministry, much less start a church in your own home, it becomes a family affair. I talked to myself in the mirror in January, my grandmother passed in July, and by September we had the first church service in our living room. Even now, writing that takes my breath away a little bit. I'll always have a special place for those 20 loyal believers who faithfully met in our living room, always.

Eventually, our home church merged with a local growing church where I served as the Missions Outreach Pastor for nearly 8 years before stepping down in late 2018, while always maintaining my secular career, affectionately known as the Insurance Job, since 2004.

Now, if you're already this far into my book, I'm shocked. I know, it's only the first chapter, right? But hey, I'm the realist whereas my beautiful bride Christy is the dreamer of the family. Much of my life I've felt God calling me to do something that seems bigger than me and I've pushed away from it because I have this fear of failure and imperfection. (That's what my counselor says anyway.) So when Christy started telling me I should write a book, just like she said I was being called to the ministry, I blew her off.

Really, what do I have to say? I'm just an ordinary guy living an ordinary life.

She agreed I'm an ordinary guy and I think even added in boring as well, but she also said, *There are people out there who need to hear that.*

My life has been anything but ordinary once I quit rejecting God's calling and allowed him to get ahold of me. Having a chance to look back at how God worked in and through my entire life, especially the last 10 or 15 years, I started to agree with Christy, but writing a book, that's a big deal! What can I say that nobody else is saying? Who will buy it? How will I get it published? After all, I had already failed at getting a children's book published years earlier. Did I mention, who will buy this thing?

Then God started knocking, again. I laid on the couch, again. I pretended not to hear, again. Then one day while in my best Jerry Clower relaxation position, with a leg propped up on the A/C as to where the cold air would blow up one leg of my pajama bottoms and down the other, I thought about Jonah. You remember ol' Jonah, right? He was that guy who God clearly told to go to Nineveh but instead he laid around on the boat heading in the other direction (see Jonah Chapter

1). Yeah, I've always had this lifelong fear of being randomly swallowed by a fish at every turn, so, I wrote the book.

By the end of this thing, I want you to have connected with me, an ordinary guy, on some kind of level that you haven't been able to connect with other people you may have seen as *religious* in the past. (I despise the word *religious* by the way. I'm sure I'll explain why in this book somewhere.) Look at me as your neighbor, coworker in the cubicle next to you at work, fishing pal, scrapbooking partner, golfing buddy – whatever a normal person is to you.

Here, let me tell you just how normal I really am. My wife Christy and I love each other deeply, and we passionately fight, often. I help drive the kids to Boy Scouts, tennis practice, and dance, and on long road-trip vacations, sometimes they vomit on me. I drive a '98 Ford Explorer with 115,000 miles because it's paid in full. It still has a cassette deck, and if I want to listen to my iPod, I use one of those cassette adapters that plugs into the earphone plug, which works brilliantly by the way. In my house, clean laundry is piled on the couch and the socks never get folded, but thrown in a basket until winter comes or Nana can't stand it any longer. The hate for folding socks is a thing in our family, and we've instilled it in our children. My house dog Annie still pees on the carpet after years of semi-successful potty training. I only say semi-successful because the *semi* part gives me hope, even if it is false, that she will get a clue any day now. I go to church weekly, but I'm not sure I can make it a day without sinning. Sometimes I take out a bad day at work on my kids, and later I have to go back and apologize. I then lay in bed hoping they will forget what a jerk I was. I cuss out loud if I smash my thumb with a hammer building a chicken coop, and I cuss in my mind at the thought of using a public restroom. That may make me more weird than ordinary, but I have this severe phobia of public restrooms. Feel like you know me better?

If you are hoping for some deep, theological revelations from this book, well, you are not going to find them here. What you will find are the lessons God has taught me through what appears to be the ordinary course of life. One of the gifts God gave me was storytelling. If you could meet or have met some of my family – namely my Grandpa Melvin or Grandpa Marcus, both now deceased – you would understand I come by this honestly. So with some present and past stories, I want to illustrate chapter by chapter what God has taught an average guy. For the most part each chapter is a stand-alone message and can be read in order. But, heck! Skip around if you'd like. Some of what God revealed was in the moment; some I've realized now looking back on life; some are just good stories that I had to find a way to share, but it doesn't mean I'm proud of all my actions. My style is honesty especially when it hurts, satire laced with sarcasm, presented alongside an occasional country embellishment that every good storyteller is entitled. Most times I'm hard on the American church and churchy religious people, but I have an overabundance of grace for those hurt by them and new believers trying to break their way into churchy America. I make zero apologies for my harshness or mercy. We stand to learn something from the faith of the third world church and the passion of new believers. If any of this has already upset, disinterested, or just plain bored you, then I'd say find a different book. If you're still with me, well, let's get started. But before we go, I want you to think as you read. I want this read to be more than entertainment for you.

Think about your everyday life and what God has been revealing all along that maybe you missed, what is He revealing now, and what would you be willing to do for God if you knew you couldn't fail?

CHAPTER 2

I HATE THIS CHURCH

God brings the right people at the right time in history to do what God wants done.[2]

Pastor Craig Groeschel

I HATE THIS CHURCH! screamed my 5 year old son Wyatt.

Not as much as your Daddy does right now, I thought to myself looking into the faces of four people, all of whom were family, sitting on my living room couch.

It was the second meeting of the church I was convinced God wanted us to start in our home. People said they would come but for whatever reason they didn't. What I found out over the next couple of years was that God always brought who He wanted and needed in this church at the right place, at the right time, and for the right message. All He wanted from me was to obey, then allow Him to do the rest.

The outcome does not matter; that is up to God. Our obedience to say and do what He is asking is what matters, and there is beauty in that obedience.

Sounds so slick and easy, right? Like a well done infomercial. Just do what He says and you'll be covered with a double rainbow, encircled with unicorns as you lie down next to a stream of strong, black coffee that you can simply dip your mug into at will. Yet here I sat with a screaming child, empty pews (a.k.a. the couch), and communion juice in the carpet. For me, what was happening in my living room was the modern day equivalent of preaching naked. Those that are close to me know this is my go-to obedience example in scripture, and one of my greatest fears. Many of you know Isaiah as our *Lord send me!* Old Testament cheerleader or the first prophet of the coming Messiah that we quote at Christmas. To me though, he is the guy that God asked to preach naked – for three years! Don't remember that from the ol' Sunday school flannelgraph do you? Well, see for yourself.

...at that time the Lord spoke through Isaiah son of Amoz. He said to him, "Take off the sackcloth from your body and the sandals from your feet." And he did so, going around stripped and barefoot. Then the Lord said, "Just as my servant Isaiah has gone stripped and barefoot for three years, as a sign and portent against Egypt and Cush, so the king of Assyria will lead away stripped and barefoot the Egyptian captives and Cushite exiles, young and old, with buttocks bared—to Egypt's shame. Isaiah 20:2-4 (NIV)

Preaching naked is a far cry from rainbows, unicorns, and steaming streams of coffee. Answering the call to start a church in your living room is pretty distant as well. So did I always hate that church? Absolutely not! The beauty in bold obedience is always there; it just takes some time for us to mature enough to see it and for the bud to blossom. God so often works through a process. I don't think of my screaming son when I think of my start in ministry, unless Christy and I are wanting a good belly laugh. No, what I think of is the feeling I had when the first car pulled up to the curb in front of our house – the first car that wasn't a family member's. I think of how excited our entire family was. I think of the haven, the place God created for those hurt by church to heal.

I think of the summer we gave away 1,000 hotdogs to hungry people in a local park. I think of one of our faithful families paying to have a green vinyl sign made with white letters that said *Free Hotdogs This Wednesday*. The sign was $80 and we got it on the cheap because the sign company got stuck with a blank green vinyl sign someone purchased and never picked up. Plus they loved the idea of us serving free hotdogs in the park. I think of a former addict/coyote/carny/drug smuggler we met while volunteering at our Community Christmas Dinner. He was interested in coming to church. Yes, the church that met in my house. The house where my family slept at night. And oh, yes, he came, drank pots and pots of our coffee while sitting on our couch, and believed in every part of our ministry! My family now proudly calls him friend.

I think of taking the time to call each member of our living room ministry when we were contacted by a young, up-and-coming church here in town that wanted to discuss a merger and of the commitment I made before I called every single person. I committed to drop the merger proposal if even a single person was not comfortable with the idea – the tradeoff was not worth the chance of losing even one. I think of the person who said, *I've never felt truly accepted in a church until I came here but you are my pastor and I trust your decision if you say this new place will welcome me too.* (Gulp!) I think of a loyal group of friends and family that believed in me at times when I didn't believe in myself. I think of obedience, and I picture each and every one of their beautiful faces.

There is beauty in obedience. The outcome does not matter; that is up to God.

Oswald Chambers once said, *If I obey Jesus Christ in the seemingly random circumstances of life, they become pinholes through which I see the face of God. Then, when I stand face to face with God, I will discover that through my obedience thousands were blessed.*

What do you hear God asking you to do that you haven't acted on yet?

CHAPTER 3

HOW YA'LL DOIN'

The proper office of a friend is to side with you when you are in the wrong. Nearly anybody will side with you when you are in the right.[3]

Mark Twain

Now, as we ease our way through this book, this is one of those stories that has parts, as in, I hope my boys and girl are never involved in any part of it. None of it! Our testimonies – the good, the bad, and the ugly – and the Holy Spirit are the greatest tools for ministering to others. There is no better way of connecting than for someone to know that we've been there too. In this particular story, the name of my friend has been changed – not to protect the innocent, but rather the guilty. I'd change my name for this story, too, but since it's in my book, well, that just doesn't make much sense.

My friend Keith and I were out one night doing some backroading in search of a little mischief. Where I grew up, backroading was an official weekend past-time that was not endorsed by parents or coaches anywhere. It was done at night, with adult beverages in tow, and on the endless dirt roads that surrounded our small town. If you weren't on the dirt roads, you were not truly backroading. Now, notice I said mischief; we weren't necessarily looking to get into trouble, just mischief. Huge difference.

So, for entertainment on this particular night, we decided to head out to our local city lake and see if we could catch some of our buddies parking with their girlfriends. Parking was not trying to find a spot to pull into at Wal-Mart. Parking was going into the country and finding a semi-secluded place to slap in the Def Leppard cassette you had copied in order to make out with your girlfriend. This, too, was not endorsed by your parents.

We eased into the city lake parking area about 5 miles from our hometown limits. Low and behold there were no parkers but there were some drinkers, and they were from a nearby rival town, Wayne. To my recollection, there were five guys all together in a tiny Toyota extended cab pickup. Now, Maysville students and Wayne students did not like each other and weren't supposed to like each other, especially if they played sports. How did we know they were from Wayne? Because one of these guys, who I still see in my nightmares to this day, was a mountain of a man. He was not a boy; he was a man, I expect working on his third or fourth year of 10th grade. He was a tall, redhead that sported a full Jeremiah Johnson beard. Once you see a guy like this in a football uniform on the opposing team you never forget him.

There they were, minding their own business, just taking it easy on the tailgate of their undersized truck as Keith and I pulled up next to them.

He rolled his window down, hung out an arm, and beckoned a friendly, *How ya'll doin'?*

That oh so simplistic question mixed with his natural charisma was just inviting enough to draw them a few steps closer to see who this cat was. Those last few steps of curiosity was all Keith needed.

He looked over at me with that infamous grin I'd seen so many times before and said, *Watch this!*

In one fluent motion, he dumped the clutch while hitting the gas pedal propelling the truck into the wickedest donut I've ever been a part of. Just as the dust engulfed us to the point we couldn't see and the rocks pinged off the sides of the truck, I remember seeing the Wayne Giant's jaw slap the ground in absolute astonishment. To this day I don't know how Keith knew which way was out as the gravel parking lot transformed into some kind of dust-nado. But, he did it; he found fresh, clear air, and a way out as I doubled over belly laughing in the passenger seat!

When I finally regained control of my bladder I looked behind us to see a tiny set of headlights waayyy back there. That's when a series of events transpired that I hope my kids never repeat. A guy in an old truck, moving along about 25 mph, pulled out in front of us. Not a big deal, right? Except Slow Poke came out of nowhere, in the middle of nowhere, and it was the middle of the night with oncoming traffic.

You people should be in bed! It's late! What are you doing out here? were just a couple of the edited comments slipping from my mouth. We could not get around this guy as the headlights behind us were getting uncomfortably closer.

By the time the road cleared, the Wayne Giant and his minions were on us, and they didn't find our mischievous act nearly as funny as we did. Honestly, we weren't finding it as funny either, and I had bladder problems for another reason now. We had just crossed over the fine line from mischief into trouble. And that trouble had just caught us from behind.

In one high speed swerve, their sardine packed pickup flew around us, with one of the minions hanging half out the window demanding us to pull over. For self-preservation, we declined and watched them go off ahead of us.

Ha, they're going on! Nope, wrong again! They had gotten far enough ahead to pull sideways in the middle of the road, completely blocking it off. There they were – all five of them – standing with arms crossed in a single file line across the road like a Dukes of Hazzard roadblock. Instinctively, we also stopped in the center of road, just out of empty bottle throwing range, to discuss our options. I immediately surmised there was no safe option other than to go back. I mean that was a pretty easy assumption to make at this point. This is when Keith decided to break the news to me we were sitting on empty; he wasn't sure we even had enough gas to get back to town.

So there we were, blocked, surrounded if you will; enemy in front, bar ditches on both sides, and not enough gas to get back to the safety of town.

Keith looked across the seat at me, *Brown, I'm getting out.*

WHAT?

Yep, I think I can talk them out of this.

WHAT???

Brown, I'm getting out!

WHAT???? Talk them out of it? Are you crazy? Have you forgotten you just cut the largest donut in recorded history on these guys? Which was AWESOME, by the way.

[insert high five here]

Thank you very much.

You're welcome.

This is why they are blocking the road, not because they want to have a Maysville-Wayne peace summit!

No, Brown, I really think I can talk them out of this.

You know, Keith, I'm pretty sure I can't whip you, but I'm willing to try if you attempt to get out of this truck. I stand a better chance of surviving you than I do those five. Does the little one have an axe handle?

Maybe...

Thought so...

Then what do you suggest I do?

Head at them fast and hard, and once they are convinced we may just be stupid enough to t-bone them, we hit the ditch and go around them.

And that my friend is just what we did. I'm not sure if their eyes were bigger when we slammed them with the donut or when they were certain they were about to be cratered as we flew into the ditch, uprooting sunflowers and part of an alfalfa patch as we were off to town, praying we had enough gas to get there.

Trying to figure out where God is in this story, yet? Well, I'm still alive to tell it for starters. The lesson I learned now looking back as an adult came to me when I was reading 2 Kings 6:13-15 (NLT). It's about Elisha, a prophet of God, who had upset a king who opposed God's people.

"Go and find out where he (Elisha) *is," the king commanded, "so I can send troops to seize him."*

And the report came back: "Elisha is at Dothan." So one night the king of Aram sent a great army with many chariots and horses to surround the city.

When the servant of the man of God got up early the next morning and went outside, there were troops, horses, and chariots everywhere. "Oh, sir, what will we do now?" the young man cried to Elisha.

Can you imagine what this cat felt like? The servant wakes up all stretching, scratching, and trying to get the junk out of his eyes. Then stumbles outside to get some water for coffee, because that's what all men of God do first thing in the morning, only to find his wake-up call to be some ticked off king's troops with horses and chariots everywhere!

Do you ever have those times in your life when you have felt this way, surrounded by the enemy? Think along the lines of times when we don't know what to do in our everyday life. When we are confused in our marriages, overwhelmed in our jobs, and the only friendships we have are on thin ice. These are times when you are surrounded.

That's how I felt that night with Keith. If I wasn't there by his side for some wise counsel, he would have done something that would have messed up his world [insert my pat on the back here]. Actually, had I not been there, we probably wouldn't have been in that pickle in the first place, but that's beside the point. Keith would have gotten out of the truck, surrounded by the enemy, and been pummeled! A good ol' fashioned country beat down.

Many times in life we feel like our enemy, Satan and his minions, have surrounded us. I've learned the deeper I go with God, the more I feel surrounded like Elisha. This is just a byproduct of a blooming relationship with our Father. The devil hates the love-filled relationship we have with God, and he will do anything within his power to stop it. He will tempt us to step off the path God has set us on, and we usually feel most surrounded when we've just started something new or feel we're on the verge of major life change.

You know those times when you've started giving up an unhealthy habit, then you encounter twice as much stress in your life that only increases the urge. Your family decides to get on a budget to create some margin and savings, only to go out and find the car won't start. You and your spouse start marriage counseling, yet you're fighting more now than before. Actually, you find yourself fighting on the way to your counseling session. You quit a hobby because you want to spend more time your kids. Now you feel you don't know them and aren't sure that they don't hate you. And you know what my friend? This all makes perfect sense. I'm not crazy! Think about it. Why would Satan be interested in us at all if we were already on a highway to hell? But take an exit on that road God is leading you down and now he takes notice. As Denver tells his friend Ron in the book *Same Kind of Different as Me, When you is special to God, you become important to Satan.*[4]

When we are alone, or at the very least feel a sense of isolation, it's so much easier for the dark side to get us to submit.

I loved nature shows as a kid and still love them to this day. So in my mind, I see this playing out like something from *National Geographic*. There we are, that lonely wildebeest cut from the herd by a pack of hyenas. That's a bad spot to be in because it never ends well for the one alone on the plains of Africa. Remember *The Lion King*? Duh! We might not literally be on a hyena's menu but we are attacked. We are brought down every day by affairs, shady business practices, overspending, anger, time away from family, addictions, depression, and whatever is going on in your life that I didn't mention. Do you feel as if you are being chased right now and your tank is running low? Don't think you can make it back to town? Feel as if your only option is hit the ditch, and that's not a very good option?

Ecclesiastes 4: 9-12 (NLT) gives us some incredible advice:

Two people are better off than one, for they can help each other succeed. If one person falls, the other can reach out and help. But someone who falls alone is in real trouble...

A person standing alone can be attacked and defeated, but two can stand back-to-back and conquer. Three are even better, for a triple-braided cord is not easily broken.

Think about it. All the greats have had a partner.

Lone Ranger had Tonto.

Batman had Robin.

Marshall Dillon had Festus.

Moses had Aaron.

David had Jonathan.

I know from personal experience how vital it is to have someone in our daily walk that we can call our accountability partner. It took desperation for me to seek out mine. It took the weight of ministry, family, and work combined for me to finally see I needed someone to trust and to hold me responsible. The words in Ecclesiastes should have been a reality to me so much sooner.

One of the greatest lies of the devil is that we can do life alone. He will convince you that life is easier without friends, a church family is way too complicated, and eventually Jesus himself has left you. Don't buy into the deception! If you will seek out an accountability partner, you will find you are not alone. In fact, not only do you have someone to tell this to, but you will find out that they share the same attacks, struggles, and temptations, and they are just as afraid as you to share with anyone. And that vulnerability matched with trust can create a lasting bond.

So, don't believe the devil's lie that you can do this alone. Find a strong trustworthy partner. We all need someone.

Do you have someone you are confident you can call without hesitation at 3 a.m.? Someone who loves God just as much, if not more, than you? If you can't answer that with a resounding, *YES,* then it's time to start praying for God to bring you someone.

The heartfelt counsel of a friend
is as sweet as perfume and incense...

Proverbs 27:9 (NLT)

CHAPTER 4

A HEART OF MERCY

When there's a need sensed by a few and each individual understands his responsibility and gives his all, regardless of the odds, then Jesus works a miracle.[5]

John Maxwell

It was March of 2002 when my beautiful bride walked into my office, visibly shaken, fell limp into my guest chair, and mustered two words from her trembling lips that would change the course of our lives forever, *Heart murmur.* She thought she was taking our six month old Winston, our first and only child at the time, to the doctor for an itchy scalp, but what he left with was congenital heart disease.

In a matter of weeks we went from an itchy scalp at our local physician's office in Enid to Children's Hospital in Oklahoma City where they performed a balloon catheter procedure on Winston's aortic valve. During the post-operative checks, they found another, more severe, problem with the aorta itself that would require open heart surgery under the world renowned pediatric cardiologist, Dr. Christopher Knott-Craig. Looking back now, I'm pretty certain we never even treated the itchy scalp. Welcome to parenthood!

Picture this, here I am this new dad with seven months of parenting under my belt waiting in Children's Hospital holding my first born baby boy in my arms. It's still a vivid memory. It was a mini waiting nook, no bigger than a small walk-in closet, with a single bench that sat just outside the stainless steel double swinging doors, the doors that led into the operating room. We stood there at a stalemate across from the nurse in her full surgical attire. I held a slightly sedated Winston in both arms with Christy by my side. The silence broke when the nurse said, *Take your time.* My twisted legalistic mind overrode my sorrow as I asked, *How long will you wait?* In a soft, sweet voice, she replied, *As long as it takes.* For some reason, I found comfort in her answer, though I desperately wanted to push the limits of its truth. Comfort and logic eventually choked out fear as I did the hardest thing I had ever done in my life – I handed over my son to this total stranger knowing full well she would disappear with him behind those stainless-steel doors. The image of Winston in her arms could have been the last one I ever had of him, and in that, there was something strangely intimate about the exchange.

We stood in the private waiting room they had assigned to us complete with *Brown Family* outside the door. Earlier the nurse found our family seated in the *normal* waiting room, as if there is such a thing when you are in a children's hospital, and explained to us that we had a private room. Seeing our name on the outside of that door, as I took a quick glance at all the other pale-faced families who weren't assigned a private room, made me realize that this thing was way up on the seriousness scale.

Dr. Knott-Craig entered before the surgery to visit with the family. In his thick South African accent, he explained the process and how each hour someone would come out of surgery to update us on Winston's condition. Before leaving he made a request that caught me completely off guard. He asked if it was okay to pray with the family before he left and informed us that he and his surgical team would be praying over *his baby* before they started. One of the many unique characteristics of Dr. Knott-Craig wasn't just the praying with families, but the reference to my child, a patient, as *his baby*. Something the staff told us he did with every baby once they were under his care. This wasn't a man with a God complex, no, just the opposite: a man full of enough of God's love and compassion that he would treat each stranger's child as if it were his own. Again, strangely intimate. I felt my wickedly high anxiety level fall for the first time in weeks. Something the meds I started were supposed to do already.

The next four hours are a bit hazy.

I remember the final update was from a surgical intern with a Duke University surgical hat, and then soon after, Dr. Knott-Craig emerged with the news that the surgery was a major success; it even took two hours less than they expected.

I remember a pastor in the room at the time using the word *miracle*.

I remember thinking there were too many pastors in the room even if it were only two.

I remember having some overwhelmingly foreign feelings and thoughts, aside from the joyous feelings of my son being alive and well, that I did not understand, but I knew they were a different kind of good. Yet, I was thinking that tossing the word *miracle* around was being overly dramatic.

Fast forward through Pediatric ICU (PICU) and the pain of seeing my child on a respirator; I want to get to the third day. This is the day we waited in a standard hospital room watching Winston sit up, unassisted, in the bed, laughing as he enjoyed his bottle while I continuously inspected the incision that ran top to bottom down his chest. I couldn't take my eyes off of it. What would life be like for us now? Day three is when Dr. Ward came in and spouted off, *If you guys lived in the metro area, I'd send you home today! We've never seen a child recover from open heart surgery this fast.* Oh to be horrified and excited all in one. I recall hearing his words and looking at the pile of luggage that contained nine to eleven days of clothes because that's what they told us to prepare for, and as I stared at that pile, I said under my breath, *Miracle.*

This was a long time ago. Year three of my marriage and year one of parenting. I can look back and say the realization of a miracle still isn't what changed me, though it was a catalyst. It's taken me all these years to process just what God was up to that day. Now I see the key is in the events leading up to us ever making it to the hospital as we received a multitude of prayer cards, some from total strangers. I remember my Aunt Ann in Tennessee letting us know they had multiple churches praying for us out east. We received a prayer cloth that my cousin had anointed and prayed over with her church. Honestly though, it meant very little to me then. I did not believe God worked that way. I appreciated them thinking of us, but I did not believe in a God that worked actively in the here and now. We were to pray because the Bible told us so, not because there was power in it.

Remember the John Maxwell quote I used to introduce this chapter? *When there's a need sensed by a few and each individual understands his responsibility and gives his all, regardless of the odds, then Jesus works a miracle.* I saw this play out right in front of me during those days in the hospital. The ironic thing is I was not one of those who understood their responsibility and sure did not give his all, but there were hundreds that did through their prayers. It took me all these years to finally see him as a God that still works miracles in the healing of kids, and in spite of the hardened hearts of fathers, he does heal just like the Bible stories I heard as a kid.

He is a God that met me where I was, in my current internal filthy condition. I was still in a time of running from Him that dated back to college. He is a God that loved me enough to be faithful to me when, at best, all I had was a token faith in Him. He is the God of Romans 9:14-16 (NLT): *Are we saying, then, God was unfair? Of course not! For God said to Moses, "I will show mercy on anyone I choose, and I will show compassion to anyone I choose." So it is God who decides to show mercy. We can neither choose it nor work for it.*

I was one of those *anyones,* and this chapter of my life is where I was changed forever. Reflecting back, have you felt the mercy of God when you weren't looking for it or when you didn't deserve it? If you let it, could God's mercy change the rest of your life, too?

CHAPTER 5

I'M GONNA GET YOU SUCKA'

...because judgment without mercy will be shown to anyone who has not been merciful. Mercy triumphs over judgment.

James 2:13 (NIV)

I was raised in the country. My heart and my roots still go back to my country upbringing. If you are with PETA or any other animal rights group, if you refer to hunters as "Bambi Killers," or if you just don't think hunting is "right," then you need not read any further because you will most likely be disgusted, appalled, and possibly insulted.

When my cousin Jarrod and I were young, we had this thing against possums. Not opossums – they only have those up north – I'm talking about possums. For the most part they were pesky! They really weren't bad but they really weren't good either. They were just always in the way when we were trapping *coons* (raccoons).

Okay, let's get this out of the way. Yes, we trapped coons! Possibly the highlight of our year as kids, very close to a Christmas morning type of experience for my cousin Jarrod and me. It was fun then, and I would still think it was fun today if my Grandpa was around to give it another go!

Every summer when it was about time to pick our Grandpa's sweet corn (and I'm not talking about a couple rows, I'm talking a couple acres of corn) we'd trap coons.

Why would we trap those cutesy, cuddly, wuddly little raccoons you ask? Because if left unsupervised, coons will DESTROY a patch of sweet corn. Something I learned very early was if there was ever an animal I believed to be schizophrenic, it's a coon! Oh yeah, they look all innocent and adorable on Marty Stopher's *Wild America*, BUT I'm here to tell you that pound for pound they are the meanest animal on the face of the earth, bar none!

Again, Jarrod and I have stories. OH, do we have stories. If you throw a bacon grease soaked biscuit in a room with a three day starved coon and a pit bull, my money is on that coon coming away with that biscuit EVERY. STINKING. TIME! Sorry had to get that last shot in; I think you get the point.

So, in the course of coon trapping, the odds were much greater that we would trap a possum rather than a coon. I don't know why. Maybe possums got an earlier start, maybe they were dumber, maybe they were smarter, maybe we didn't know what the heck we were doing, but inevitably we would catch about 10 possums to every one coon. It would just tick us off, but possums had to be "taken care of" as well because they could damage the crop too, though not as bad. If we let them go, they would just keep getting back in our traps over and over and over, so it was "dirt nap" for them without a second thought.

Fast forward to this present day...

My family came rolling into our driveway here in Ada and looked up to see, YES, a possum eating our cat's food. Something else I never understood about possums is they are never in a real hurry to get away if they even try at all. They just waddle around, act real mean, hiss a lot, and look like something God threw together on the 24th hour of the sixth day of creation with a bunch of leftovers.

I immediately threw the car in park, and my old childhood instincts kicked in. I had flashbacks to being a kid again, listening to Jerry Clower records, and Uncle Buddy telling some outlandish story about hook men and hungry panthers to keep us scared all night while we were checking coon traps!

In my mind I'm thinking...

Dude (possum) you're toast!

I've hated your kind since I was a kid.

I hate you to this day.

You picked the wrong bowl of cat food today bro!

So I jumped out of the car, which my beautiful bride quickly locked me out of, and walked straight up to the possum, looked him in his hideous face, glanced at the shovel that was propped up against the wall AND I... scooped him up and harmlessly pitched him over the fence.

Christy let me back into the car and, knowing me better than anyone, said, *I figured you were going to smack him with that shovel. Why did you just throw him over the fence?*

Somewhat confused myself, I replied, *I don't know. I've become more merciful in my old age I guess.*

What I really meant to say was, *I've grown more merciful and forgiving the closer I have grown to the One who forgives me.*

Did the nasty love child of a raccoon and skunk deserve to die? Heck yah!

Was the filthy retch doing me dirty? Heck yah!

Everything about me would normally say, *Smack that sucka' in the head, the arrogant fool is eating it right in front of you no less, HE DESERVES IT!*

But the more I go through life and realize how jacked up I am and how I mess up every single day and how God still forgives me even when I don't deserve it – the more I feel compelled to hand out mercy and forgiveness. Sometimes even to my old nemesis, the possum.

The more time I spend on this earth, the more I am overwhelmed with gratitude for Romans 5:8 (NLT): *But God showed his great love for us by sending Christ to die for us while we were still sinners.*

It did not say, God sent his son to die *for us because we deserved it.*

It did not say, God sent his son to die *to show the greatest act of forgiveness and mercy the world has ever seen because we were good people.*

It says, God sent his son to die *WHILE WE WERE STILL SINNERS!*

I used to be the world's worst at holding grudges. If Guinness had a world record for it, I'm positive I would have been in the book with a picture of me and my Beaver Cleaver plastered comb over hairdo holding a list as long as my arm. When I first met my wife back in college, I seriously had a "list" of those who I was not only NOT going to forgive, but I was actually going to get revenge on sometime before I died. This is no lie!

But the more God and I walked together, the more he helped me realize, *Man, I am still a sinner! I use and abuse God every day, and every day he still forgives me! That's the best deal going! Not only forgives me but He throws my mess out into the Sea of Forgetfulness. So who am I to decide who gets forgiven in my life?*

I read these words once and this topic became as real for me as anything I had ever been convicted of. When we refuse to forgive, what we are saying is *God, I don't trust you to do your job, and I can it better.* If you could use OUCH and WOW in the same sentence, I did!

I finally trashed my list and oh what a relief! Like an Alka-Seltzer after a third bowl of crawfish étouffée. It was a weight removed from around my neck. Truly liberating!

Then I started to feel the gratitude the Psalmist felt in Psalms 130:3-5 (The Message) when he said,

If you, God, kept records on wrongdoings,

who would stand a chance?

As it turns out, forgiveness is your habit,

and that's why you're worshiped.

Who do you need to scoop up with the shovel and pitch over the Fence of Forgetfulness?

Who's the possum in your life? He or she has a name.

It's time to tear up that list.

CHAPTER 6

BOOTS AND BOTTLECAPS

Indeed, if we consider the unblushing promises of reward and the staggering nature of the rewards promised in the Gospels, it would seem that Our Lord finds our desires not too strong, but too weak. We are half-hearted creatures, fooling about with drink and sex and ambition when infinite joy is offered us, like an ignorant child who wants to go on making mud pies in a slum because he cannot imagine what is meant by the offer of a holiday at the sea.

We are far too easily pleased.[6]

C.S. Lewis

The Board of Fame is a cloth-covered corkboard in my office filled with tacked up quotes, pictures, scripture, key chains, and other "fame worthy" items that I have collected since graduating from college and entering the working world full time back in 1998. One of the items that had marinated on the board for a while was an advertisement for a pair of caramel colored full quill ostrich Tony Lama boots. Yes sir, I had big plans with the next raise, promotion, or when I had finally "arrived" to buy those boots for myself! The ad served as a sense of inspiration I guess, but with each raise or promotion life happened – a new baby, a house, four-door car, dog needs spayed, septic tank just backed up into the master bath, etc. Thus, the boots remained on The Board.

Then in 2012, life just didn't happen. A complete life change happened! Africa happened. Yes, I'm fully aware Africa has always been there, but it wasn't until then that God sat Christy and I on a plane and sent us across the globe to be matched up with our 5 year old daughter Akosua, aka "Zoey," in Ghana some 3,000 miles away. Jumping through the frustrating adoption hoops with our guides, we spent three weeks there. Our guides, Peter and Anna Osei-Kwame, who were also Godparents to our daughter and had both grown up Ghanaian orphans. As aggravating and lengthy as the process was, it allowed for us to soak in Zoey's culture, spending time in her village, in African church, and with the people on the street and working in the hotel. It allowed us to steep in our daughter's beautiful culture for just a little while.

We returned back to the states leaving Akosua there, as we knew we would. The purpose of our trip all along was to meet our daughter, go through Ghanaian court to be granted custody, and submit all the required documents to the American Embassy in Ghana in person. Now back in Ada, Oklahoma sitting at my desk, I found myself daydreaming about our very first meal with Zoey only hours after we first met. The restaurant was just around the corner from the local government offices in the city of Kumasi. We entered through an unpainted, rusty screen door into a room about as big as an American den where you'd find a family watching TV together; that was the whole place in its entirety. The room was lit only by what came in the door and windows, no a/c, six or eight wooden tables, and, somewhere in the background, an African soap opera blared – there's always an African soap opera blaring in the background. This was the place that *Kumasi government employees ate their food, and it could be trusted on an American stomach,* Peter told us. He ordered us a round of Coca-Cola that came out in old school tall glass bottles with pop-off caps. We quickly grew to love Kumasi with their buildings and structures still resembling the 1950s when Ghana won its independence from Great Britain. I vividly remember us sitting at that table, waiting on our Red (beans) and fish, watching Peter and Zoey play an African kids' game with bottle caps on the table. Nothing goes to waste in their culture, right down to the bottle caps. It made me think of my Grandpa Melvin and the time he showed how they made cars and the girls made dolls out of dried corncobs when he was a kid growing up on the farm during the Depression.

I shook off my office daydream, looked up on The Board of Fame, walked over, took down the ad for boots, and threw it in the trash. The emotions that started at that restaurant table continued on through the weeks we spent in Ghana inflicting a painfully humbling perspective on my very American life. I was reminded of this quote from C.S. Lewis, which also resides on The Board:

Indeed, if we consider the unblushing promises of reward and the staggering nature of the rewards promised in the Gospels, it would seem that Our Lord finds our desires not too strong, but too weak. We are half-hearted creatures, fooling about with drink and sex and ambition when infinite joy is offered us, like an ignorant child who wants to go on making mud pies in a slum because he cannot imagine what is meant by the offer of a holiday at the sea. We are far too easily pleased.

I can't tell you the exact thought that was going through my mind when I decided to trash my dream boots, I just reacted. If you've ever spent any time in a third world country as an American, you know that you are immersed in events and images you'll have to mentally shuffle and sort upon your return. This process lasts for months, or even years. For me, the reality of being far too easily pleased kept punching me in the gut like the schoolyard bully you regrettably pegged in the face during a round of 4th hour P.E. kickball.

The vivid images of my daughter's village, where she continued to live until moving into our home, and the old school Coca-Cola bottle caps she used as toys kept spinning in my head. Believe me, there's a lot of room up in this empty head for spinning to happen!

Confused thoughts about my boots and her bottle caps consumed me until I came to this obscure conclusion, *Zoey and I both are too easily pleased!* Yes, I said both of us! And before you call me a heretic for having said this about my formerly orphaned child, let me explain. Understand that two completely different character traits caused this. I am easily pleased due to my American comfort and entitlement while she's easily pleased by her innocence. In my entitlement and comfort, I am the *half-hearted creature(s), fooling about* and she in her innocence wants to be a part of my world. So here we are both making mud pies in a slum together. I say this because during our stay together, at 5 years old, she uttered these words in her native Twi, *I am ready to go. There is nothing for me here.* And as I pondered those words I desperately wanted her to understand, *Baby, don't be so easily pleased. There is nothing for you here either, but there is a holiday by the sea waiting for us.*

Now, here is the part where after you've read my previous statement you're confused, convicted, upset, or I've already lost you, but you're hanging in because you're my aunt, and you want to squeeze my cheeks at the next holiday and tell me that you read my book. Nonetheless, I've said this before, and I'll say this again – America cannot, did not, and will not fix my daughter! If you don't understand that statement, then honestly you have the wrong idea for God's calling to international adoption. No problem, I didn't fully understand either until I specifically prayed for God to open my eyes and heart to adoption.

It is true that God, by His will, has chosen us to be born and to live in this great country. America has given us opportunities and has provided us a means to be a loving forever family to a fatherless child half a world away. But simply bringing her here to our land of luxury did not fix her! She did not need fixed! She was not broken! She was perfectly made in the image of God, just like me! What was broken were her circumstances, being left in life without a mother and father. Now that could be fixed!

But herein also lies the flaw in my previous conclusion. I actually thought when she cried out, *There's nothing for me here* that she desired an upgrade from Ghanaian bottle caps to American boots. And I honestly laid in bed preplanning about how I would protect her from my American materialism. Then as He had done so many times, God humbled me through a child when He whispered to me, *Wake up Tyson. You make proclamations you don't even understand yourself! She gets it. Arrogant boy, her cry is not for your spoiled country. She knows about the real holiday by sea far more than you because I have clothed her in innocence and it protects her from your simple-minded selfishness. Son listen, her cry is a yearning to share this journey to the sea with you, her father. Now, wake up!*

Waking up humbled again, I see her through His eyes. Now, I see she and I aren't making mud pies in the slum together. Nope, it's just me, with a mud pie in one hand digging through a trashcan looking for a picture of my boots with the other. She's already traded in her bottle caps while I still stand here far too easily pleased.

What has you far too easily pleased? I hope I don't look over to find you sitting in the mud next to me...

CHAPTER 7

MAN IN THE MIRROR

As you grow older, you'll see white men cheat black men every day of your life, but let me tell you something and don't you forget it – whenever a white man does that to a black man, no matter who he is, how rich he is, or how fine a family he comes from, he is trash.[7]

Atticus Finch, *To Kill a Mockingbird* by Harper Lee

What business did a white middle class family of four have hanging out in a tiny, two-bedroom low-income apartment with a single black mom and her five kids listening to a busted iPod that only had one song, Michael Jackson's "Man in the Mirror," on Thanksgiving? Honestly, they had no business blessing us with that time in their home at all, but they did.

That day will always be etched in my mind.

God, in his divine wisdom, allowed our paths to cross months earlier when I called a friend who ran a local community outreach center and asked him if there was a family our home church could assist and build a relationship with. As for names, we'll call her Dee. And God knew my family needed Dee more than she needed us. Growing up white middle class in rural Oklahoma, I had my tainted, naïve, and preconceived notions of what poor African American life was like. Honestly though, I had never, ever spent relational time with any African American, much less a single mom with five kids. She too had notions about what the inner-workings of a white middle class family looked like but had never spent any time there either. Yet here we were: all nine of use crammed into a loveseat and small couch that myself and a group of friends had carried up her stairs and dropped in her tiny living room a few months before when we first made our introductions.

She was braiding her daughter's hair when all these *white folks* showed up with an overwhelming amount of donated home furnishings. It was the only way we knew how to help. She kept on braiding the hair and didn't say 10 words. Just kept on braiding. It was the only way she knew how to say thank you. At the time, I thought she was ungrateful. I didn't understand her, nor she us. At the time she thought we were well-to-do whites just getting our gold star for helping a black family. But again, here we were watching her three youngest kids in a dance off as "Man in the Mirror" played over and over again.

Finally, one of us felt comfortable enough to ask a question. Then another trickled out from the shy shadows of curious hearts. The comfort level rose and so did the boldness of the questions. Before the night was over, we were in a full blown Q&A session you might title *What White and Black Folks Think about Each Other.* This was a conversation you could and should have only after a relationship has been built. (The last sentence is a warning to you if you're white and have a black acquaintance you like to refer to as your *black friend.* If you have to add the *my black friend* phrase in every time you refer to that person, then you shouldn't insult them by trying to have that conversation. You don't have a relationship, and you don't get it.) That night was the true beginning of a racial awakening for me. One that has not stopped, and I can't seem to get enough of it. This somewhat innocent Thanksgiving night would change my family's life – and mine – forever.

You see, throughout the course of this evening, both families realized no matter how friendly we all had been up to this point, we had serious preconceptions and stereotypes of each other that had been handed to us from generation to generation. Our limited interaction and surface level relationships with each other's race had us biased from the beginning. And from my white perspective, the generational sin of white on black racism that's been allowed to be handed down from generation to generation, has skewed my view of race as much as anything else. The excuse for both families: *it's all we knew.*

So why do I say we needed her more than she needed us? We never expected that within the next 12 months God would lead us to Ghana, Africa through the process of adoption. His prompting led to a little girl that my world, specifically the American world, sees as black, surely not African, possibly African American, but most certainly black. She'll be seen in a way I can never truly relate to or feel except for the 20 days Christy and I spent as the minority in her Ghanaian homeland. Twenty days is not even a taste of exposure. My 20 days in the span of her lifetime is about as equivalent to one of Abraham's descendant sand grains falling on the sea shore. Our adoption case worker said to Christy and I before our departure to meet Akosua, *You guys soak in these next few weeks. Take it to heart and try never to forget. Because for the first time in your life you are a minority, and for 20 days you will feel what your daughter will feel the rest of her life so long as she stays on American soil.* She was right. Other than my brief but cherished days in Africa, I don't have any idea what it's like to be a minority, much less an impoverished minority in America. But for a season, we were allowed a glimpse into that window of life as Dee shared her home with my family. We talked openly and candidly and belly laughed out loud together as we shared why our races do what they do. Dee had no idea what she was prepping us for, and we had no idea either. I'll always remember that Thanksgiving and what God was up to. I'll always be thankful for Dee opening my eyes and heart by allowing us into her life and home. She broke down stereotypes and barriers that paved the way for God to bring a little African girl into my life, as my daughter, and give me just a tiny, tiny understanding of what life feels like for her.

My feelings on this chapter may be best summed up in the words of Latasha Morrison from the Be a Bridge Builder movement. Latasha says in a social media post, *Even with the best of intentions, when you tell us you're colorblind, you're communicating that you can't (and don't want to) see us. You don't want to acknowledge our differences. Our skin, our color, our preferences, our culture, etc., are a part of who We are. God created diversity and He called it good. Saying you're colorblind makes us feel like you're making us look like you, the white majority. But the best that we can be are the individuals God created. He could've made us more like you, but He chose to make us instead. We are all part of His creation. So let's celebrate the diversity among us, and live the gospel TOGETHER as God designed.*

God created diversity and called it good. What a beautiful sentence! Do your eyes need to be opened to see the diversity God created and to see His goodness? Romans 13:11a, 12 (NIV) says, *The hour has already come for you to wake up from your slumber...So let us put aside the deeds of darkness and put on the armor of light.* Ask God to wake you up! Even if you think you are awake when it comes to race, especially if you're white, I promise there is more to be revealed than you think.

Have your eyes been opened to even a hint of racism within you? Where does this prejudice originate – home, work, society, your own heart? Ask God for guidance, forgiveness, and grace as you begin to acknowledge others' differences and celebrate the diversity He created.

CHAPTER 8

T-SHIRT TO TUXEDO

You are valuable because you exist.
Not because of what you do, or what you have done,
but simply because you are.[8]
Max Lucado

Son, what is that you have on? were the first words that came from my mouth at 7a.m. one weekday morning when, The Middle, Wyatt walked into the kitchen dressed and ready for 4th grade picture day.

Dad, it's what I'm wearing to school, he replied as I looked over his haphazardly put together ensemble of wrinkled t-shirt, shorts, and colored athletic socks hiked to mid-shin.

Well buddy, it's picture day, I said.

I know, Wyatt responded with zero emotion.

Now we're interlocked in this long but not awkward pause, because we've done this so often, staring at each other, me giving him every possible chance to realize there's substance behind my question and statement. Several moments passed and still no response, only a blank stare that said, *Uh, what are you getting at Dad?*

Wyatt, it's picture day. You need to go and put on something decent.

Why? You and Mom never buy them anyway.

[me, clearing my throat]

This is true son, but this picture will go in your school's yearbook, and your mom and I want you to look presentable. We'd like for people, at least for today, to think that we actually do purchase clothes for you from time to time that weren't from the lost and found of a junior high locker room. Yeah, that one generated some zero to sixty emotion in less than a second as he flung around and stomped off to his bedroom, shutting the door behind him saying something under his breath that I'm positive I would have punished him for.

I went to discuss the wardrobe malfunction with my beautiful bride who was getting ready in our bathroom. As soon as I walked in, *You need to remind Wyatt it's picture day and he needs to wear something decent.*

Oh, I did already.

What did he have on?

Wrinkled t-shirt, shorts, and socks that could be spotted from the International Space Station.

He can't wear that!

I know. I've already sent him back in to change.

I went back into the kitchen to finish up the morning routine of coffee, kids' lunches, dishes left in sink from the night before, and general prodding of anyone under the age of 13 to keep the process moving. When somewhere in the distance, I hear the rumbling of ZZ Top's "Sharp Dressed Man" as Wyatt emerges from the bedroom with almost ironed khakis, a button down shirt, and a bow tie.

Back to the bathroom to my bride I go.

Well, did he change?

Yep. T-shirt to tuxedo.

Huh?

T-shirt to tuxedo. You know Wyatt, there is no in between. It's all in all the time. Once he makes up his mind he's gonna own it. He's wearing slacks, a button down, and bowtie.

Christy and I were recently reminiscing on this story when she commented, *Isn't that really how God sees us? We see ourselves as the wrinkled t-shirt, but God sees us as His perfect creation already in our full glory clothed in righteousness as His beloved.*

Think about it. Like Wyatt, there is no in between with God. There is nothing we can do to make him love us anymore extravagantly than he already does. Our job is removing as many obstacles as possible in our life to get as close to Him as we can. And when we do, the more we start to understand, and the more we understand, the more we become this unstoppable Gospel machine. As Graham Cooke says, *No one will be safe from a blessing.*[9]

But you are a chosen people, a royal priesthood, a holy nation, a people belonging to God, that you may declare the praises of him who called you out of darkness into his wonderful light. 1 Peter 2:9 (NIV)

For he chose us in him before the creation of the world to be holy and blameless in his sight. Ephesians 1:4 (NIV)

How do you think God sees you? As a kid in the wrinkled t-shirt or in a tuxedo, clothed and ready for picture day? How can you embrace the belief that you – just as you are – are God's perfect creation clothed in righteousness?

CONCLUSION

Now this is not the end.
It is not even the beginning of the end.
But it is, perhaps, the end of the beginning.[10]
Winston Churchill

So how do you conclude a book made up of a bunch of stories? I guess you tell a story about the man who taught you to tell stories one last time. In my Grandpa Melvin's final years, his hearing deteriorated to the point that he couldn't hear me on the phone any longer. Living in a different town with a busy family, ministry, and separate full-time job, I just wasn't good about getting back home to visit as much as I had in years prior. I started to carry some guilt about my lack of presence, so I did what I knew how to do: I wrote. I wrote him a letter every couple weeks. I'd update him with what all was going on with our family, tell him a funny story, of course, include a few pictures, and I eventually started including a short devotion about something I had learned from God or how our church and ministry were doing. I felt compelled to add the devotion because I really didn't know where he stood with the Lord and his salvation which had burdened me for some time even though he often told me how proud he was that I was a *preacher*. It's funny how the hardest people to talk to about salvation are often those that are closest to us.

After many months of writing one-way letters, I decided to send one that included a self-addressed stamped envelope and an offer for him to write me back if he so desired. Maybe, just maybe, this invitation would give him a non-intimidating opportunity to ask me any questions he may have about God or salvation or life ever after.

What I received a few weeks later was not what I expected, but it came in true Melvin fashion. A summons, I've now come to call it, to come over to his house and *stay all night,* the equivalent of a sleep over. My journal entry from May 9th of that year says it best, *Grandpa wrote me back a letter. Said he wanted to spend some time with me. Said we had a lot to talk about. I don't know what he wants, but I wrote him back and told him I was coming over this weekend to stay all night. I really don't know what to expect, but I know he said he is growing old. I hope he answers God's knocking if he never has.* I prayed the rest of that week for God to give me an opportunity to talk to him about this salvation. God answered, and he did not disappoint.

I rolled up to his house about dark and through the window could see him sitting in his spot at the table, worn linoleum under his feet and cigarette in hand. As I walked in, the coffee was made and the reason for the summons unfolded immediately. I no more had the duffle bag off my shoulder when he had me a cup poured, and the first words from his mouth were, *Well Tyson, I'm about ready to go see your Grandma. Don't know how much longer I'll be here.* Honestly, I grinned with my back to him and mumbled under my breath, *Well God, I asked for an opportunity. No sense in wasting time, right?* I picked up the dry erase board that we used to communicate with. He could still hear my voice even with his bad hearing, but I didn't want to mess this chance up. I scrawled, *So is your heart right with God?*

What happened next was one of the most unexpectedly beautiful things I've ever witnessed in my life. I watched my white haired grandfather, who I'd never seen enter a church, sit there in his overalls and push through the tears as he recited the entire 23rd Psalm from memory without a single hesitation or pause for recollection. I felt physically lighter with each tear as I wiped away the previous question from the board to replace it with the statement, *You are ready.*

He then informed me to get some *shuteye* that we'd be *hittin' it at first light in the morning.* A phrase that all of us grandkids knew oh so well. We had a lot of work to get done because we were going to find every home-site he ever lived on before that Saturday was over. He said, *Tyson, I want you to write a book about me someday. You think I'm worthy of a book don't you?*

4 a.m. came way too early. And a little too early for a heaping plate of sausage, eggs, toast, and coffee. He woke me by asking if I was planning on sleeping the day away and informed me that breakfast was ready. Out of respect and kindness, I forced it down. A thermos of coffee was filled to the brim and off we went. We were at the first home-site, his birth site, before *first light.* A gate was open and unlocked, so

there we were driving through a dark pasture behind someone's house before daylight as he continuously reassured me it was okay; he knew right where he was going. I had no doubt he knew right where we were. I was more worried about the possibility of trying to convince the homeowner of that while looking down the barrel of a 12 gauge. But if we did, it wouldn't be the first time he had gotten us in a pickle, but it could be the last, so I went with it.

That Saturday adventure took us to 17 home-sites in over three counties. I was blessed to see the pond where his father and sister were baptized, two locations where he nearly drowned, the spot where he was standing the day they first heard Pearl Harbor had been attacked, the place he lived when he was turned down the second time trying to enlist, and I even heard the shame he experienced going into town knowing others his age were fighting and dying, yet he was never given the opportunity to do either. We also visited the pickle shack, the schoolyard where he and his brother tag teamed a bully on their first day at a new school, the trees (that are still standing) they dug from a nearby creek and replanted at their school on the first Arbor day, the house they lived in when he contracted polio, the home near his where a murder occurred, the field they would run through swatting bumble bees with paddles made from broom corn slats to pass the time, and the cellar door that hail stones beat holes through. Story upon story upon story was told that day, waiting for a time to be shared again.

And just when I thought an old dog couldn't learn a new trick, my 89-year-old grandpa asked if I'd ever eaten at a Chinese buffet, *When you want more you just go up there and get a brand new plate as many times as you want!* To top it off, you'll never guess what my fortune cookie said: *You have a charming way with words, you should write a book.* I can't make this stuff up! Yes, Grandpa you are worthy of a book, but for now the best I can do is a little of the beginning and ending of my first one.

If you've hung with me this long, I want to close with a single piece of advice that I hope you might remember even if you don't take anything else from this book – Don't miss a chance to listen. I'm not speaking of a chance to hear, but rather a chance to listen.

Don't miss a chance to listen to your spouse if they see something special in you that you haven't or won't. Don't miss a chance to listen to what God is telling your children because it's usually more honest and genuine than we jaded adults will ever know. Don't miss the chance to listen to the nothingness of a quiet house and the chaos of kids, friends, and dogs when they burst from that same nothingness. Don't miss a chance to listen when your Grandpa asks you to *stay all night* one last time. Whatever you do, don't miss a chance to listen.

EPILOGUE

Eight years! That's how long it took me to get here. That just goes to show you what some pure and simple fear of failure will get you if you really put your mind to it. I am no longer in the ministry, not in a formal corporate role. After 10 years, God spoke clearly when He said that job for him was done. I stepped out of my role as a pastor and into a more present role as husband and dad.

THANKS

Noelle, your time spent on this work in exchange for coffee until 3 a.m. and a horse trough are not nearly enough. I needed someone who got me and would be brutally honest. Fortunately and sometimes unfortunately, I got both. Remember the "Grandma's prayer journal" comment? It's been such a blessing to Christy and I that this turned into much more than just "a book" work. If this thing doesn't sell a single copy, it has been worth the friendship it created. Blessings, our friend.

NOTES

1. Max Lucado, The Applause of Heaven: Discover the Secret to a Truly Satisfying Life (Nashville, TN: Thomas Nelson, 1990, 96, 99)

2. Craig Groeschel, Network Summit, 2011

3. Mark Twain, as quoted in R. Kent Rasmussen edited, The Quotable Mark Twain: His Essential Aphorism, Witticisms, and Concise Opinions

4. Ron Hall and Denver Moore with Lynn Vincent, Same Kind of Different as Me: A Modern Day Slave, an International Art Dealer, and the Unlikely Woman Who Bound Them Together (Nashville, TN: Thomas Nelson, 2006)

5. John Maxwell, sermon, Problem or a Miracle, Life.Church, 2012

6. C.S. Lewis, The Weight of Glory and Other Addresses (New York, NY: Simon & Schuster, MacMillan, 1980, first publication 1949)

7. Harper Lee, To Kill A Mockingbird (New York, NY: Harper Collins, 1960)

8. http://www.azquotes.com/quote/544017

9. Graham Cooke, The Favor Series, cd

10.Winston Churchill, The Lord Mayor's Luncheon, Mansion House, November 10, 1942

AUTHOR BIOGRAPHY

Meet Tyson Brown, a country raised, science educated, ministry chosen storyteller from Oklahoma. A seemingly average family man doing life in rural southern Oklahoma when a flippantly uttered birthday comment – I'm 33 today. Jesus was 33 when he died. What have I done to make His kingdom bigger? – leads to a series of events that will alter his path forever. Only months later he realizes he's been called by God to ministry, a world he never asked to enter but reluctantly accepts as he attempts to still maintain his secular career. Tyson finds out that not only has he been hearing God now, but he has been hearing God all along. This awareness causes him to see God intimately in the stories of his ornery youth and even in the lively family he's currently raising –

from the creek bottoms of Oklahoma to the plains of West Africa. Whether it's late night grace exhibited to a possum in his own driveway or the unrest in his heart as he wrestles with the thought of his daughter's transition from life in a Ghanaian village to America, God's been breathing into it. All of it. All along. Tyson uses his unique storytelling talent to unlock the reader's ability to hear God and challenges them to act in every chapter. Tyson Brown delivers you a whimsical, raw, challenging, humorous, authentic journey.

Made in the USA
Coppell, TX
05 December 2022